THE

MNA

LISA

MYSTERY

THE MONA LISA MYSTERY

Timothy Knapman

Illustrated by
Pedro Rodríguez

Collins

Contents

The Louvre museum and the Mona Lisa

Chapter 1

My dad used to say, "Every great painting is also a great puzzle." When I asked him what he meant, he told me about his favourite painting. It was of a woman called Lisa del Giocondo, and every time he looked at it, he said, her smile was different.

"How is that possible?" I asked him. "I don't know, but it's true." This was in 1911, and by then, the painting was nearly 400 years old.

As it turned out, that painting was the cause of the greatest puzzle my dad was ever asked to solve.

But I'm getting ahead of myself.
First, I should tell you that here in France,
we call the painting *La Joconde*, which
means "the happy woman" but you may
know it as the *Mona Lisa*. It hung in
the Louvre Museum in Paris, and it was my
dad's job, as head of security, to make sure
that it stayed there.

It wasn't just the *Mona Lisa* that Dad
had to look after. The Louvre houses some
of the world's greatest art, so he was
very busy.

The museum was closed on Mondays,
but every other morning, at 9 o'clock sharp,
he would tour the whole building.

He checked the locks and the windows. He made sure that his guards were in their places. Like a general inspecting his troops, he even checked their buttons were bright, and their boots were polished.

Some days, like the one I'm going to tell you about, he took me into work with him. Fathers didn't spend much time with their children in those days. Instead, we were expected to find things to do. They thought that would teach us to look after ourselves. I don't know if this was right; all I know is that I enjoyed the time I spent with my dad. I was very proud of how important he was, striding through those splendid rooms, past those grand paintings, being saluted by men in uniforms.

I remember that Dad would often point out something interesting as we walked.

For instance, one day he nodded towards a shadowy corner, next to a window.

"You see that statue over there, Madeleine?" he asked. (I should have said that my name is Madeleine; his name was Gabriel, Gabriel Falaise.)

"Yes, Papa," I replied. Peering into the gloom, I could just make out a statue of a boy.

"Bring it to me," he said.

It looked too heavy for me to lift but I knew my dad would have a reason for asking, so I went over. I reached out my hand, only to discover – to my surprise – that it wasn't a statue after all: it was a *painting* of a statue.

"It's what we call an optical illusion," Dad explained. "The painter has used his skill to make the statue look as real as possible. The light from the window next to it gets in your eyes so you can't see as well as you might. Your brain does the rest. You've seen statues in corners in other rooms in this building, so your brain expects to see a statue here. And that's what you see."

9

"What lesson does this teach us? Always look closely at things because appearances can be deceptive. Will you remember that, Madeleine?"

I nodded solemnly and, as you will see later, I remembered the lesson.

My dad always followed the same route through the museum, finishing his tour in a grand room called the Salon Carré. This was where the *Mona Lisa* hung, and my dad always took time to look at her. He said it was his reward after that long tour of the rest of the museum. Nowadays, the *Mona Lisa* is the most famous painting in the world, and you have to queue to get even a glimpse of it. Back then, however, it was less well known, and my dad didn't have to wait to get the painting to himself.

But, on this particular morning – Tuesday 22nd August 1911 – things were different. Instead of the painting, the only things to be seen were the four iron hooks from which it usually hung.

Dad summoned the guard.

"Where's it gone, Pierre?" he asked.

"Another gentleman was just asking me that, sir," Pierre replied. "He was here with his sketchbook, wanting to make some drawings. I said I haven't seen it this morning. Perhaps it's been taken to be photographed for a new postcard or to go in someone's book."

Without another word, Dad grabbed my hand, and we went marching off.

He pushed through a door marked "Private" and we clattered down a shabby staircase to the museum's workrooms. These were where the pictures were taken to be cleaned, restored and – sometimes – photographed. Dad grumbled that people had no business taking things from the galleries without asking him first.

When we reached the workrooms, however, no one had seen the picture either or had any plans to photograph it.

"It can't just have vanished into thin air!" Dad snapped. He ordered a thorough search of the entire museum. All they found, stuffed behind a bin, were an empty frame and the glass case that had recently been fitted to protect the painting.

That was when we knew for certain.
The *Mona Lisa* had been stolen.

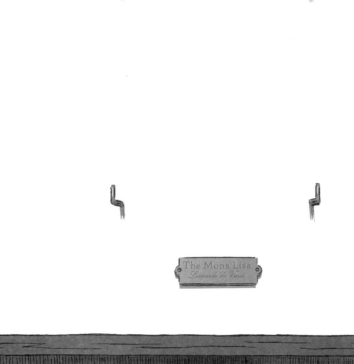

The Mona Lisa
Leonardo da Vinci

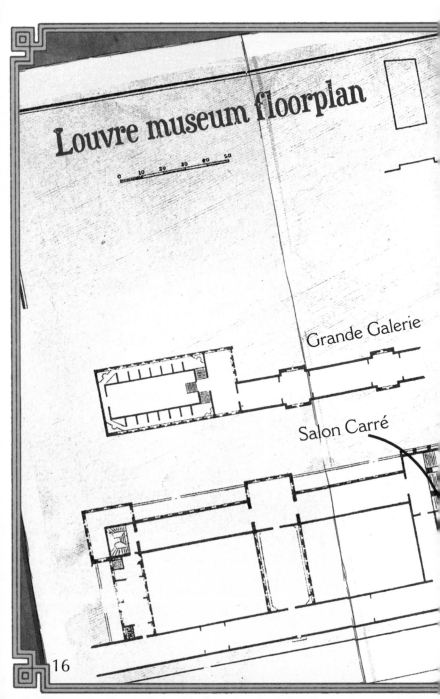

Louvre museum floorplan

0 10 20 30 40 50

Grande Galerie

Salon Carré

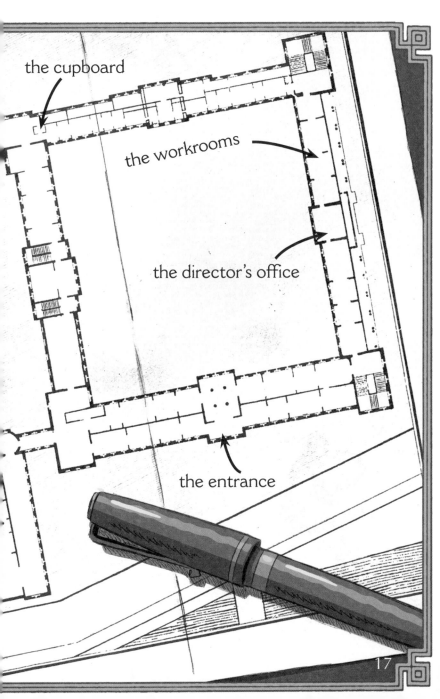

the cupboard

the workrooms

the director's office

the entrance

17

Chapter 2

"If they can steal the *Mona Lisa* from under our noses, they can steal anything!" thundered the director of the museum.

We were in his office, watching as he paced up and down, getting more and more agitated. "The moment the press gets hold of this, we'll be a laughing stock! We must get her back! There is not a minute to waste! The honour of France is at stake! What shall I tell the president?"

"You can tell him that we have the situation under control," said Dad. He was a practical man. This was just another problem that he had to solve; all he had to do was think about it logically.

"Here are the facts as we know them," Dad began. "The *Mona Lisa* was still hanging in the museum last thing on Sunday evening – Pierre, the guard, swears to it."

"The guard?" snapped the director. "What use was he? It was *his* job to stop it being stolen!"

"With respect," said my father, "this museum has 400 rooms and only 200 guards, with fewer guards at night. We're closed on Mondays and the painting was not there first thing this morning. Therefore, the theft could have taken place at any time between closing time on Sunday night and opening time on Tuesday morning."

Dad thought for a moment before he went on: "Whoever did this is clever – very clever. After all, they've just stolen the *Mona Lisa*! They will have taken it as soon as possible after we closed on Sunday evening. That would give them the maximum amount of time to get the painting out of the museum and far away from here before anyone noticed."

"I will call the chief of police!"
said the director. "I'll get him to close
the borders!"

"I'm afraid it's already too late for that,"
said Dad. "The painting probably left
the country yesterday."

"No!" Despairing, the director collapsed
into his chair.

My dad, by contrast, left that office looking determined.

"You must go straight home, Madeleine, and don't dawdle. Do you understand?" he said. "We're going to close the museum and I'll have to interview every member of staff who was here on Sunday. Tell your mother I've no idea when I'll be home tonight."

The closing bell was ringing as I made my way through the museum. Wherever I looked, guards were ushering visitors to the exits.

No one knew about the robbery yet, so people were complaining as they left: since when did France's greatest museum suddenly close in the middle of the afternoon?

People from the workrooms were milling around in the emptying galleries, waiting to be interviewed. They all wore loose white smocks to keep their clothes clean.

"Madeleine!" one of them called out to me. "What's all this about?"

He was Italian with a splendid, waxed moustache. His name was Vincenzo Peruggia and he worked at the museum doing all sorts of things, from framing pictures to fixing leaks.

Vincenzo was my friend. When Dad was busy with work, he'd send me off to find something to do, and I'd often bump into Vincenzo. Vincenzo read a lot of books and he was always telling me stories about the building and the pictures – especially the Italian ones. If he thought I needed cheering up, he'd invent games for me to play. That wasn't something my dad would ever do. My favourite were the treasure hunts, when he'd hide paintbrushes for me to find. There were so many nooks and crannies it took me ages to find them.

"You still have one paintbrush to find!" Vincenzo said.

"Sorry, Vincenzo," I replied, "but my dad says I must go straight home and no dawdling."

"And the head of security's daughter always does what she's told," said Vincenzo. I wanted to go anyway, I was getting hungry and Vincenzo was waving his sandwich around and it was making me even hungrier!

"What's that delicious smell?"

"Food," Vincenzo said. "*Italian* food, not that creamy nonsense you French are always going on about."

"'Creamy nonsense?'" I couldn't believe my ears. "French cooking is the finest in the world!"

Vincenzo laughed – he liked to tease me – and he waved the sandwich around a bit more. I had a choice: walk away and preserve the honour of French cooking or grab the sandwich and take a bite. I grabbed the sandwich. It was wonderful: crusty bread, pickles and … what was that special taste?

"Fennel," Vincenzo explained. "We use it a lot in Florence, the city in Italy that I come from. You can have another bite if you like … " I made a lunge for the sandwich, but he lifted it high out of my reach, "… once you've told me what's going on."

"Can you keep a secret?" I asked. He nodded, so I went on. "You know the *Mona Lisa*?"

"Of course," he replied, rolling his eyes. "Lisa del Giocondo was also from Florence, don't forget. Only the other day, I fitted a glass case on that painting to protect it."

"You needn't have bothered," I whispered. "It's been stolen."

Rather than looking surprised, Vincenzo nodded his head thoughtfully for a few seconds, then he said, "Well, it's about time."

Chapter 3

I must have looked shocked because Vincenzo burst out laughing. Then he said, "I'll explain. Let's take a walk."

"If you promise my dad won't catch me," I said. "He told me to go straight home."

"I promise," he replied.

As we went from room to room, Vincenzo didn't mention the pictures on the walls. Instead, he pointed out the beautiful decorations – the marble stairs, the fine ceilings, the carvings on the wooden doorframes.

"You know the Louvre didn't start off as an art museum."

"No, you told me," I said. "It was built as a royal palace."

"And then, a little more than a hundred years ago, you French decided you'd had enough of royalty," Vincenzo went on. "You got rid of your kings and queens and turned this palace into an art museum. Art connects us to our past, to beauty – to our most important feelings.

"Everyone should be able to share its power, not just a few people with crowns on their heads.

"In fact, the only problem with your revolution was the revolutionaries," Vincenzo went on. "They talked about liberty, equality and brotherhood but couldn't stop killing each other, until none of them were left. Then a general took over, named Napoleon Bonaparte, and for nearly 20 years, there was no peace in Europe.

"Some say that Napoleon tried to conquer the world for the glory of France – I say rubbish!" Vincenzo sneered. "It was for his own glory. You know he even renamed the Louvre the 'Napoleon Museum'? The nerve of the man!"

We were back in the Salon Carré – the room where the *Mona Lisa* had hung.

"Napoleon got married in this room," said Vincenzo. "He dared to call himself an emperor when he was nothing more than a murderer and a thief. He plundered other countries and dragged their treasures back here!"

Vincenzo's moustache twitched with fury. My friend was usually the happiest, kindest person but I could see he was angry.

"Even in my beloved Italy – the birthplace of the Renaissance, that great flowering of all the arts – nothing was sacred, not even the greatest painting of them all, Leonardo da Vinci's *Mona Lisa*!"

"You're telling me the *Mona Lisa* was only in the Louvre because Napoleon stole it?" I asked.

"How else do you think it got here?" said Vincenzo. "It didn't walk all the way from Florence."

At that moment, he heard something and held up his hand. There were footsteps in the corridor outside, and voices talking.

"It's Dad!" I gasped. "He told me to go straight home! What am I going to do?"

"Hide, of course!" said Vincenzo. "After our treasure hunts, you'll know all the best places."

The *very* best place to hide in the whole of the Louvre (if you ever need to – I hope it's still there) was a mop cupboard three rooms away from the Salon Carré. The cupboard was in a corner and made of dark wood, so no one ever noticed it (unless they needed a mop, I suppose). The door handle was so stiff, you needed two hands and a lot of determination to turn it. Most people would just assume it was locked and leave you alone.

Except that on this particular day, the door handle wasn't stiff. I gave it a good twist and it turned so easily that I nearly fell over. Someone had oiled it.

Who would bother doing that?
Before I could think any more about
that, I heard my father's voice saying,
"In here, gentlemen." They were coming
into this room! I pulled the cupboard door
open and slipped inside. Dad and his guards
were just outside! I held my breath.

"Gentlemen," I heard Dad say. "I have no doubt that the theft of the *Mona Lisa* was the work of a master criminal. This robbery is a masterpiece and the thief may well never commit another crime. That means we have only this one chance of catching them. The whole of France will be willing us on, and I know that, together, we shall succeed!"

There was applause and cheering. They wouldn't be able to hear me, so I started to breathe normally again. That's when I realised there was a smell in that cupboard – a wonderful, delicious smell – and it reminded me of something. Before I could work out what it was, the noise outside died down as the room emptied. When I was sure I was alone, I slipped out of the cupboard and made my way home.

Walking through the sunny streets of Paris, I felt very odd. I was worried about my dad – how would he ever catch a master criminal? – but there was something else too. That wonderful, delicious smell had somehow given me a very strange idea. I shook my head. It was ridiculous – impossible! - and by the time I got home, it had slipped my mind entirely.

Chapter 4

The Louvre stayed closed for the rest of
the week. Inside, my dad, his guards, and
the best detectives on the Paris police force
worked day and night. My mum had her
own theories. She sent me to the museum
with food every day to keep an eye on my
dad and the investigation. She wanted to
know all the details. That was how I was
one of the few people who actually got
to see the investigation as it happened.
I remember going in that Wednesday and
seeing the wall around the four iron hooks
covered in powder. A detective in overalls
was carefully flicking at it with a brush.

"Is he brushing away all that mess?"
I asked.

"It's not mess, Madeleine," Dad explained to me as he ate his way through the picnic basket I had brought. "It's the latest thing in crime detection. That powder picks up the marks people make with their fingertips – what we call 'fingerprints'. Everyone's fingerprints are different, so this will tell us who touched the wall around the *Mona Lisa*."

"Including the thief?" I asked.

"Precisely," Dad nodded. "The problem is that, although we tell everyone who works here to use gloves, they almost never do, so there are lots of different fingerprints. Even the man who put the glass case around the painting left his fingerprints behind!"

Dad finished his meal and put the picnic basket to one side. "This thief is even cleverer than I thought. Every day I check every window and every lock, but I haven't found any signs of a break-in. Nobody saw the thief enter the museum or leave with the painting."

"It wouldn't be that hard to get the painting out," I said. "Once the thief had got the glass case and the frame off, it would be easy to roll the canvas up and hide it under a coat."

"Except that the *Mona Lisa* isn't painted on canvas," Dad explained. "It's painted on a plank of wood; it's not big, but it's an awkward shape, and quite heavy. No, whoever did this is a magician. It is as if the thief and the painting vanished into thin air."

By then, news of the *Mona Lisa*'s disappearance was everywhere. France was in shock and determined to do anything to get it back. Everyone leaving the country was having their luggage searched.

A generous reward was offered for information about the robbery, but nothing was found, and no one came forward.

Soon, my father gave up trying to work out *how* the thief had done it, and instead decided he would catch the thief if he could find out *why*.

"That's easy," I said. "The painting's worth a lot of money. He'll sell it and make a fortune."

"But that's just it, Madeleine," he replied. "He *can't* sell it. The painting is too famous.

"If it's put up for sale anywhere in the world, we'll know at once and he'll be arrested. He can't make any money out of this unless – " my father had an idea. "Unless someone very rich paid him in advance. The thief would then pass the painting on, and it would disappear into the very rich person's private collection."

"But the very rich person would have to keep it a secret forever," I replied. "They could never show it to anybody; never share it with anybody." I remembered what Vincenzo told me about art belonging to everyone.

"Very rich people often don't like sharing," my dad said darkly, "and they have lots of secrets."

"Maybe the thief didn't steal it for money," I said, remembering the way my dad felt about the painting. "Maybe the thief stole it for love."

The newspapers had plenty of ideas, but they didn't bother checking if any of them were true. One said the leader of Germany had done it to embarrass the French government.

Another said the painting had been spotted in Japan, then Russia, then Brazil. Alongside each story, they printed a photograph of the *Mona Lisa*. Millions of people who had never seen, or even heard of the painting were suddenly fascinated by it.

THE CAIRO BULLETIN

(EXCLUSIVE SERVICE OF THE ASSOCIATED PRESS.)

CAIRO, ILLINOIS, WEDNESDAY, AUGUST 30, 1911.

THE CRIME OF THE CENTURY

POLICE REMAIN BAFFLED

IS SHE LOST FOREVER?

When the Louvre finally reopened, something very odd happened. For the first time in the museum's history, people actually *queued* to get in – thousands of them! And what did they want to see? Not the many beautiful pictures that were still there, that was for sure. They were only interested in looking at the empty space on the wall where the *Mona Lisa* used to hang. It sounds silly, but getting stolen was what made the *Mona Lisa* the most famous painting in the world.

The investigation continued, of course. They say as many as 60 detectives worked on it, but the only detective I cared about was my dad. He never stopped trying to crack the case, but there were no fresh clues. He just kept going over the same material again and again to see if there was something he'd missed.

Dad still made his tour of the museum every morning, and sometimes I'd go with him. He walked with a stooped back now, as if he was carrying a heavy burden, and there were black marks under his eyes from lack of sleep. The guards always saluted him as he passed, but it felt like it was more out of sympathy than respect.

Eventually, a picture by Raphael, another Italian painter, was hung in the *Mona Lisa*'s place. I suppose I should have forgotten all about it then, but I just couldn't. If no one else was going to do it, I would have to solve the *Mona Lisa* mystery myself.

49

Chapter 5

Two years passed. Now and again, someone would come up with a theory and the search for the painting would resume. The director of the museum got it into his head that this was all a prank, the work of mischievous people who wanted to make fun of the stuffy old museum. He had a poet arrested, but the police found no evidence against him and let him go.

I read my dad's notes, but I knew he was a better detective than I. If *he* couldn't work out who the thief was, *I* certainly couldn't. Instead, I tried to think about the problem in a different way. I studied the history of the painting.

The Mona Lisa – one book told me – *was painted in the early 1500s, in the city of Florence.* Of course! That's where Vincenzo came from. I wished I could share my thoughts with my old friend, but two years after the robbery, he'd gone home. *Leonardo was about 50 years old when he began work,* the book went on, *but he still had the painting in 1515 when …* What I read next made me drop the book in astonishment.

I fell to my knees and picked it up again to make sure my eyes weren't playing tricks on me … *he entered the service of the King of France. The King bought the painting after Leonardo's death in 1519.*

Vincenzo had been wrong. The painting hadn't been stolen by Napoleon; Leonardo himself had brought it to France!

Something clicked in my brain. I found myself thinking of a freshly oiled door handle and a delicious smell. These things had once given me an idea so impossible that it slipped my mind almost immediately. Then I remembered the day in the museum when my dad told me to bring him the little statue, and I discovered that it wasn't a statue but a *painting* of a statue. What did he say back then? "What lesson does this teach us? Always look closely at things, because appearances can be deceptive."

Dad was at work, but I couldn't wait till he came home, so I ran all the way through Paris, into the Louvre and up the stairs to his office. I was panting when I burst through the door.

"What's the matter?" he said, looking up from his desk. His face still looked grey and tired.

"It's about the *Mona Lisa*," I said between gulps of air.

"No, Madeleine, please. I don't want to talk about that anymore."

I shook my head, "The thief! You always said the thief was clever. 'They have to be clever; they've just stolen the *Mona Lisa*!' That's what you said. You *expected* the thief to be clever, just like I expected that statue to be a statue."

"What statue?"

"It doesn't matter," I went on. "What if the thief *wasn't* that clever? What if they *weren't* a master criminal and instead the whole thing was based on a misunderstanding? You've been trying to work out the brilliantly clever way they got into the museum, but what if they didn't need one?"

"I don't understand what you're saying," replied my poor dad.

"What if the thief was there *already*? What if the reason why no one noticed the thief was because they saw him every day?"

"Please, Madeleine, I'm trying to understand but you're not making it easy."

"What if the thief worked at
the museum? At closing time that Sunday,
instead of going home with everyone else,
he hid in a cupboard.

"He knew the best place to hide because of all the treasure hunts he'd invented for a bored little girl. He oiled the handle because he had to slip in and out of the cupboard quickly. While he waited there, he ate a sandwich so delicious that the smell of it still lingered days later! All he had to do was wait for the guards to move out of the Salon Carré. Then he could step out and take the *Mona Lisa* without anyone seeing."

My father was deep in thought, testing every step of my theory as I explained it to him. "How did he get out of the museum with that heavy wooden painting?"

"Like everyone who works in the museum, he was wearing a loose white smock. The painting would easily fit under there.

"Now, a guard might spot a museum worker leaving the Louvre in the middle of the night and search him. That's why he went back to his hiding place with the picture and waited. The next morning – Monday morning – the museum is closed to the public, but the staff still go in. There would be nothing odd about him being there. He could leave without being noticed."

"That's *how* it could have happened," said my father, nodding, "but you still haven't explained the *why*. Why take these risks – especially if he wasn't a professional criminal? Did he intend to sell the painting and make his fortune?"

"No," I said. "He stole the painting for love."

When my father and I arrived home – both of us out of breath this time – I told my mother my theory.

"That's brilliant!" she exclaimed.

"Come on! Get packed!" my father laughed. "I'm going on holiday with the two people I love most in the world. We're going to Florence!"

Chapter 6

For an art lover, the city of Florence
is paradise. Its museums, palaces and
churches are home to some of the most
important paintings and statues ever made.
My father and I, however, had only one
painting on our minds, and it wasn't on
show anywhere. We paid a visit to every art
dealer in the city.

"I wonder if you could help me?" my
father would ask. "I'm looking for an old
friend who recently moved back here.
He might have come in, asking for
work as a picture-framer. His name is
Vincenzo Peruggia."

Each time, however, they would shake their heads. I began to think that this was all a wild-goose chase, and I hadn't solved the mystery after all. Our last visit of the day was to a man called Mario Fratelli.

63

Fratelli also said he didn't know
any Vincenzos, and we were about
to leave, but I was so desperate I said,
"Have you had anyone contact you out
of the blue recently? Someone offering
something special, only they can't tell you
what it is, you have to come and see it?"

Fratelli reached into a drawer. "How did you know? Why, only this morning I had this letter from a Mr Leonardo – "

That was all I needed. I grabbed the letter and ran.

"Hey, come back!" Fratelli shouted.

"We'll return the letter to you, I promise!" said my father as he ran after me. "What are you doing?" he gasped, when he caught up with me on the street outside.

"I'm sorry but look at the name on the letter: *Leonardo* Peruggia! Vincenzo's using an alias, and what better than 'Leonardo'? There's an address too."

"We must tell the police!" said
Dad, urgently. He was about to set off, but
I stopped him.

"What if I'm wrong?" I said. "I'm just
a child after all. If we call them and it's all
nonsense, you're the one they're going to
blame – unfairly – and I don't want to put
you through any more of that."

"But you're *not* wrong, Madeleine," Dad
smiled, and he put his hand on my shoulder.
"You're my daughter and I am so proud
of you."

"You are?"

He nodded. I blinked away tears.

"Well then," I said gruffly. "Vincenzo is
my friend. Let me do the talking."

Dad came with me to a dingy little house in a poor part of town.

The room was at the top of some rickety stairs. I knocked on the shabby wooden door.

"Who is it?" said a voice I recognised at once.

"It's me, Vincenzo," I said. "Madeleine."

Vincenzo opened the door. He looked as grey and tired as my dad had been.

"I knew this day would come. I'm just glad it's you. How did you work it out?"

"I smelled fennel in a broom cupboard," I said, "and I know you love your country."

"Do you want to see the painting?" he asked.

Vincenzo pulled a big case out from behind the sofa. I looked around at the peeling wallpaper and the dirty carpet. It was an odd place to find a masterpiece. The case seemed to be empty, but then he opened its false bottom and there was the *Mona Lisa*. "This magnificent work of art has been in here for the last three years," he said.

The painting shone like a light in that dark room.

"It's so beautiful, isn't it? Everyone should be able to see it, not just kings, or emperors – or thieves. Oh Madeleine! I was so eager to bring it home, I didn't think about what to do when we got here. I wrote to Signor Fratelli – he knows the director of the museum here, the Uffizi. I thought he would know what I should do."

"There is only one thing you can do," I said.

Vincenzo nodded and burst into tears. I thought of all the trouble he had caused my dad and everyone else but, looking at him, I couldn't feel angry.

"Oh Vincenzo, I'm so sorry!" I said.

At Vincenzo's trial, he said that he had taken the picture for the honour of Italy. For a while, he became a national hero, and he spent only a few months in prison.

The *Mona Lisa* was exhibited for
a short time at the Uffizi in Florence
before it was returned to the Louvre on
4th January, 1914. From then on, it was
indisputably the most famous painting in
the world.

My father continued to make his daily
tours of the museum, but when he reached
the Salon Carré, he no longer looked at it.
He told me once that he felt that Lisa del
Giocondo's smile had changed yet again.
Before the robbery, he thought she had
smiled kindly at him. Now he felt there was
an accusation behind the smile, as if she was
disappointed in him for not having found
her sooner.

I wonder how Lisa del Giocondo will look
at you when you get to see the *Mona Lisa*.

The painting is still in the Louvre, behind bulletproof glass now, and guarded by the best security system money can buy – and it's not going anywhere.

The Mona Lisa – a timeline

June 15th 1479 –
Lisa Gherardini is born
in Florence, Italy.

1479

1495

March 5th 1495 – Lisa marries
Francesco del Giocondo, a cloth
and silk merchant. They have
five children: Piero, Piera,
Camilla, Marietta and Andrea.

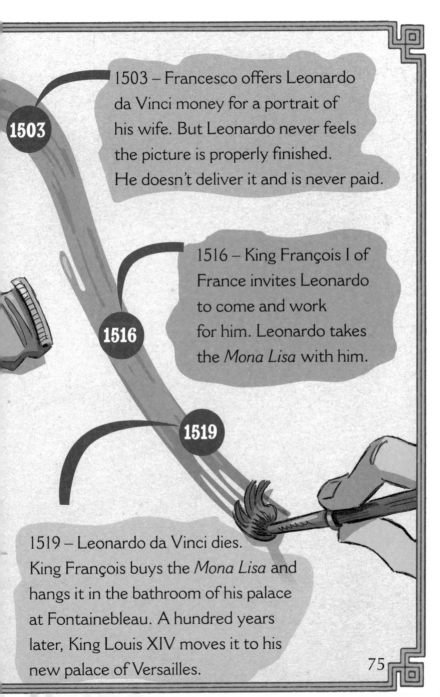

1503 – Francesco offers Leonardo da Vinci money for a portrait of his wife. But Leonardo never feels the picture is properly finished. He doesn't deliver it and is never paid.

1503

1516 – King François I of France invites Leonardo to come and work for him. Leonardo takes the *Mona Lisa* with him.

1516

1519

1519 – Leonardo da Vinci dies. King François buys the *Mona Lisa* and hangs it in the bathroom of his palace at Fontainebleau. A hundred years later, King Louis XIV moves it to his new palace of Versailles.

75

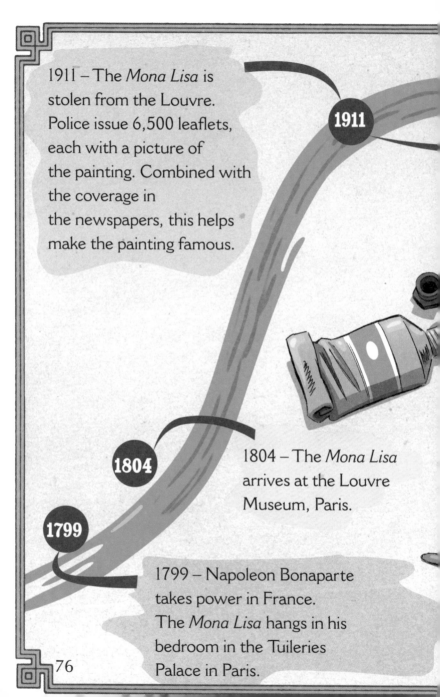

1911 – The *Mona Lisa* is stolen from the Louvre. Police issue 6,500 leaflets, each with a picture of the painting. Combined with the coverage in the newspapers, this helps make the painting famous.

1911

1804

1804 – The *Mona Lisa* arrives at the Louvre Museum, Paris.

1799

1799 – Napoleon Bonaparte takes power in France. The *Mona Lisa* hangs in his bedroom in the Tuileries Palace in Paris.

A week after the painting disappears, the Louvre reopens and people queue to look at the empty space where the painting used to hang.

1913

1914

1913 – After the arrest of Vincenzo Peruggia, the *Mona Lisa* is shown for a few months in the Uffizi Gallery in Florence.

1914 – The *Mona Lisa* returns to the Louvre Museum.

The mysteries behind the mystery

The Mona Lisa *Mystery* is inspired by true events, but I have changed a few things here and there. For instance, Madeleine and her family never existed; I made them up because I wanted to tell the story from a child's point of view.

As I was reading about the case, however, I noticed that there is a lot of disagreement about what actually happened: there are plenty of loose ends and bits of the story that don't quite fit together.

Over the next few pages, I will share different accounts of what happened, and you can make up your own mind.

Why Did Vincenzo Do It?

At his trial in 1913, Vincenzo said he was a patriot, and he stole the *Mona Lisa* to bring her home to Italy. However, in December 1911, a few months after the robbery, he wrote to his father: *I will make my fortune, and this will arrive in one shot.* In a letter of 1912, he wrote, *Live long and enjoy the prize that your son is about to realise for you.*

So, was Vincenzo's real motive to make his fortune by selling the painting?

The great escape

The Great Escape!

How did Vincenzo escape?

My sources reveal that Vincenzo was about to leave the museum with the painting when he found the door locked. He put the painting down and unscrewed the doorknob with his screwdriver, but it was no good – he was still stuck and, worse, he could now hear footsteps approaching! It was one of the museum's plumbers, a man called Sauvet. Sauvet didn't notice the picture but took pity on Vincenzo. He helped him out by opening the door with a pair of pliers.

Was Sauvet in on the crime? No one has ever found any evidence of it. All we know is that when Sauvet was shown pictures of the Louvre's employees, he did not identify Vincenzo as the man he had helped.

What could this mean? Was Sauvet mistaken or in on the plan all along?

Petty Thief ... Arrested!

28 August 1911

Petty thief, Honoré Joseph Géry-Pieret, has been arrested for the theft of the priceless *Mona Lisa*. He is friends with the notorious revolutionary poet Guillaume Apollinaire, who has called for the Louvre to be burnt down, so police believe they must have planned the robbery together.

Police have also arrested a 29-year-old Spanish painter called Pablo Picasso. Picasso is another friend of Apollinaire and had bought two statuettes that Géry-Pieret had previously stolen from the Louvre, so they are probably all in it together. They have yet to be charged.

About the author

Why did you want to be an author?

You're going to spend a lot of your time as a grown-up doing your job. So it's important to pick a job that involves doing something you love. I love stories, I always have – in books, in films, on TV, in comics, wherever I can find them. So what better job for someone who loves

Tim Knapman

stories than writing them? It's wonderful fun.

How did you get into writing?

I started writing stories at the same age as everyone else – in class, in primary school. All the other children in my class stopped writing as they grew up, but I kept going. That's how you become a writer: you keep writing.

What is it like for you to write?

Writing can be the best fun in the world – when it's going well and the ideas are flowing – and it can also be a bit of a grind when you're stuck. If you're not careful, you can think about things too much and that can make you gloomy, which doesn't help.

So whenever I get stuck, I go and do something else – it doesn't matter what – and stop thinking about my story problem. Before long, the solution pops into my head.

What is a book you remember loving reading when you were young?

My favourite picture book was *Where The Wild Things Are* by Maurice Sendak. When I was a bit older, I read all the *Doctor Who* books I could get my hands on, many of which were written by Terrance Dicks.

Is there anything in this book that relates to your own experiences?

I like paintings and going to art galleries – but I've never stolen any famous pictures! (At least, not that I'm going to tell you about.)

What do you hope readers will get out of the book?

I hope they will enjoy trying to solve the mystery alongside Madeleine. I also hope that it might get them interested in paintings and art galleries. They are wonderful places and full of stories like this one, you only need to go looking for them ...

About the illustrator

A bit about me …

I studied illustration at the Fine Arts
School La Llotja in Barcelona, Spain.
I've illustrated over 40 books. I live
next to the beach, close to Barcelona,
with my wife Gemma and my
daughter Maya.

Pedro Rodríguez

What made you want to be
an illustrator?

I don't know for sure. Drawing is something I've enjoyed
since I was very young, although I didn't know it could be
a profession. When I was little, I used to draw all the time,
read comics and novels – I've just kept doing it!

What did you like best about illustrating this book?

Everything. It's an event I already knew about, and
I enjoyed it. I also love the period in which it takes place
and trying to convey its essence.

Is there anything in this book that relates to your
own experiences?

Yes, I'm a museum thief too! Ha ha ha! Seriously, I know
Paris, the Louvre, Florence … I've always been keen on art.

How do you bring a character to life in an illustration?

First of all, I imagine them alive in my head. I often stand in front of the mirror and rehearse the poses and faces they should have. I also try to capture the character of each one.

Have you ever visited the Louvre and seen the real *Mona Lisa*?

Of course!

Did you have to do any research to get things like clothing right in this story?

Indeed, I always do! Searching for reference documentation is one of the steps and the one I enjoy most. Although, the setting for *The Mona Lisa Mystery* is a historical period I'm passionate about and I already have a lot of information.

Do you enjoy illustrating historical stories? Why?

I love history, research, and looking for documentation. I find it more interesting than drawing the modern world with its modern cars and mobiles phones. The beginning of the 20th century is one of my favourite historical periods, so I had a really good time working on this book!

Book chat

Is there a villain in this story? Explain your answer.

Does the book remind you of any other books you've read? How?

If you could ask the author one question, what would it be?

What did you think of the book at the start? Did you change your mind as you read it?

Do any of the characters remind you of someone you know in real life? If so, how?

Would you like to travel back in time to when this story takes place? Why or why not?

If you could talk to one character from the book, who would you pick? What would you say to them?

Do you think any of the characters changed between the start and end of the story? If so, how?

Which scene stands out most for you? Why?

Book challenge:

Draw a portrait of someone and try to capture their 'Mona Lisa' smile.

Collins
BIG CAT

Published by Collins
An imprint of HarperCollins*Publishers*

The News Building
1 London Bridge Street
London SE1 9GF
UK

HarperCollins*Publishers*
Macken House,
39/40 Mayor Street Upper,
Dublin 1
D01 C9W8
Ireland

10 9 8 7 6 5 4

ISBN 978-0-00-862484-2

Download the teaching notes and
word cards to accompany this book at:
http://littlewandle.org.uk/signupfluency/

Get the latest Collins Big Cat news at
collins.co.uk/collinsbigcat

Author: Timothy Knapman
Illustrator: Pedro Rodríguez (Astound
   Illustration Agency)
Publisher: Lizzie Catford
Product manager: Caroline Green
Series editor: Charlotte Raby
Development editor: Catherine Baker
Commissioning editor: Suzannah Ditchburn
Project manager: Emily Hooton
Content editor: Daniela Mora Chavarría
Copyeditor: Catherine Dakin
Proofreader: Gaynor Spry
Cover designer: Sarah Finan
Typesetter: 2Hoots Publishing Services Ltd
Production controller: Katharine Willard

Collins would like to thank the teachers and
children at the following schools who took part in
the trialling of Big Cat for Little Wandle Fluency:
Burley And Woodhead Church of England Primary
School; Chesterton Primary School; Lady Margaret
Primary School; Little Sutton Primary School;
Parsloes Primary School.

Printed and Bound in the UK using 100% Renewable
Electricity at Martins the Printers Ltd.

MIX
Paper | Supporting
responsible forestry
FSC™ C007454

This book contains FSC™ certified paper
and other controlled sources to ensure
responsible forest management.

For more information visit:
www.harpercollins.co.uk/green